PENDULUM MAGIC

AN ENCHANTING SPELL BOOK OF DISCOVERY AND MAGIC

Fortuna Noir

WELLFLEET
PRESS

Introduction

Since ancient times, people have been using pendulums to solve problems and answer questions. Pendulums have been used to locate water, lost objects or people, and uncover hidden information—a process called *dowsing*. You'll see this term frequently throughout the book.

Magical pendulums can be made of wood, crystals, or any other material that isn't conductive. Metal pendulums, for example, aren't ideal because they pick up on the electromagnetic waves in the area and are more susceptible to give a false reading. The right material depends on what you want the pendulum to do. Although crystals accept and release energy, they make a great pendulum material because they can enhance whatever spell you're performing. For example, if you want to glean an unambiguous answer, use clear quartz. If your question concerns relationships, use rose quartz. As you construct your pendulum, use a string or cord that's about 8 inches (20 cm) long and an object that's ½ to 1 inch (1 to 2.5 cm) in size so it swings freely.

In order to properly use a pendulum in your practice, you must cleanse it of all other energies. There are several ways you can do this. The first method is to let the pendulum sit in a bowl of salt overnight, discarding the salt after cleansing. Another is to pass it through incense smoke or a salt spray. And another yet is to wash the pendulum under natural, running water or with moonwater—that is, water that has been under moonlight for a full night. Last, you can hold the pendulum in your clenched hand, close your eyes, and imagine a blue flame burning and purging any lingering energies.

Once you've cleansed your pendulum, it's time to learn the proper mental state and posture in order to get the most accurate readings. Remember that your pendulum connects to your intuition and amplifies it. This means you need to be emotionally centered. To achieve this, you can do a short meditation, perform a grounding spell, lie down and close your eyes, or send a prayer to Spirit or your deities. You want to be neutral so that you'll be open to any outcome your pendulum might bring. You'll also want to be laser-focused on your question. Take several deep breaths to recenter and clear your mind of all distractions. Then, have your question clear before consulting your pendulum.

The next step is to ensure that your legs and arms are not crossed as you work. Just like cutting off circulation, this posture cuts you off from the pendulum's flow of energy. Have your feet firmly planted on the ground to connect with the earth. When using the pendulum, place your elbow on the table you're working on and use your thumb and forefinger to hold the pendulum chain. Do not let your stomach or other hand touch it. If you're standing up, make sure your arm is straight out in front of you, at a 90-degree angle from your body, to open up your posture as much as possible.

To learn your pendulum's responses, begin by holding the pendulum cord between your forefinger and thumb. Let the pendulum hover over your open palm and wait for it to stop moving. Once it's still, ask your pendulum aloud to show you the answer "yes." Do the same for "no," "maybe," and "unknown." Typically, *yes* is a back-and-forth motion, *no* is side to side, and *maybe* might be a circle.

After establishing which movement indicates specific answers, calibrate your pendulum by asking simple questions that you already know the answer to, such as, "Is today Tuesday?" See what the pendulum says. The answers might be a little off at first but keep at it until the pendulum is tuned to you and you can clearly identify answers. If you're not quite comfortable yet just using your palm, you can create a Yes/No Chart by dividing a piece of paper into three sections and writing the words Yes, No, and Maybe within each section. As you start your practice, you should ask questions with simple answers. The best way to structure your questions is to phrase them so that the answer is yes, no, or maybe. For example, "Is it better for me to stay in my current home instead of looking for another place to live?" Keep the questions focused on *you* and what you should do.

Over time, you will move away from your palm or the Yes/No Chart and dive into more detailed pendulum charts. In Chapter 1, we will cover the different types of pendulum charts and how to use them for your purposes. While you may be asked by others to obtain answers to their questions, it is important to remember not to ask questions for anyone without their consent.

As you flip through the pages of this book, you will learn to unlock your pendulum's potential as well as your own. The time to consult the Divine is now.

SO MOTE IT BE.*

* The term "So mote it be" used within is a ritual phrase historically used by Freemasons, and currently used by Neopagan practitioners translated to mean "so it must be."

1
Pendulum
Charts

TOWARD THE BEGINNING OF YOUR pendulum journey, you may find that its limited range of responses with just your palm is enough for you, but as you become more practiced, you might desire more complex answers. Not everything can be solved with a simple yes or no. That is where charts come in.

A pendulum chart is essentially a layout of predetermined answers for your pendulum to work with. Some are composed of the core answers—yes, no, maybe, unknown—and others can represent numbers, colors, affirmations, or chakras, to name a few, that each have their own meanings. You can make a chart with fabric, wood, cardboard, or anything that isn't conductive. If you choose, you can buy premade charts at a metaphysical store to get you started, but the best way to infuse your energy is to make your own. Before you begin using your chart, make sure to ask your pendulum if now is a good time to dowse. If yes, then take several deep breaths to clear your mind, put yourself in the proper posture, ask your questions aloud, and focus solely on them.

There are different types of charts you can make and different ways to interpret them. When asking your pendulum questions, make sure you always phrase them so that they are specifically relevant to you. Now, let's get creative!

DIY Charts

While mystical stores often sell pre-made pendulum charts, a good way to make a chart specific to your purposes is to simply make your own. Doing so inherently infuses the chart with your energy, so it is already attuned to you. Magic is all about intention, and your intention will be woven into every customization you make. There are three types of starter charts you can make: simple, cardboard, and wooden.

Simple Chart

A Simple Chart is just that: simple. It requires few materials and can be used immediately after being made.

Gather:

♦ Paper
♦ Scissors
♦ Colored pencils, markers, or crayons
♦ Computer and printer (optional)

First, decide whether you want the chart to be a complete circle or a semicircle. The benefit of a circular chart is that it allows the pendulum to swing according to its natural motions. It's all-encompassing. The benefit of a semicircle is that you can narrow down your answers to just a few, producing more succinct answers.

If you'd like, you can find a circle or semicircle online, print it out, and fill out the answers yourself. Or, simply cut a circle out of a piece of paper, draw each wedge, color code them, and then fill each space as you like. For example, you may want each wedge to represent yes, no, and maybe to create a Yes/No Chart. Or you can be more specific; for example, listing the days of the week. When finished, you can laminate the chart for durability.

Cardboard Chart

Cardboard is a common material that can be repurposed into a pendulum chart. Look for a piece of cardboard that's wide and long enough to encompass all the pendulum answers you need comfortably. You don't want them too close together, or you may not be able to tell which answer your pendulum is hovering over. When done properly, your chart can be just as stunning and effective as any premade chart, if not more.

Gather:

- ♦ Cardboard
- ♦ Scissors
- ♦ Printed washi tape (found at most craft stores)
- ♦ Paper
- ♦ Colored pencils, markers, or crayons
- ♦ Transparent tape

1. Place the printed tape strategically around the cardboard piece, using it to decorate and create a border. Make sure to cover every corner with it to give the surface a uniform look. If you can't find washi tape, it's perfectly fine to use your creativity with your pencils, markers, or crayons.

2. Cut the paper into a circle or semicircle.

3. Draw wedges, color them, and label them to suit your needs.

4. Use the transparent tape to adhere the chart to the newly washi-decorated cardboard.

5. Tape the answers down with the transparent tape.

After everything has been secured, your chart is ready to go.

Wooden Chart

The wooden chart is the sturdiest of them all. It's a natural material that will have a more long-lasting feel once you've finished customizing it. Here, you will use carbon paper to trace the design you want onto the wooden square. There is a lot of room for creativity because you can use multiple media to get the look and feel you want, making this chart truly unique to you.

Gather:

♦ Computer and printer
♦ Carbon paper (available at most craft stores)
♦ 8 x 8-inch (20 x 20 cm) plywood craft square
♦ Tape
♦ Pen
♦ Colored pencils, markers, crayons, or paint (optional)
♦ Woodburning kit (optional)

Create your own design—or find one online that pleases you and print it out on carbon paper. Tape the carbon paper to the piece of plywood so that the design doesn't move while you're tracing. Use a pen to carefully draw over the design. Remove the paper, and use either the paint, markers, or woodburning kit to finalize your design. Go as wild or as tame as you'd like. This is for your use only, so let those creative juices flow.

From this point on, you can use any of these methods to create the charts listed in this book or any other you come up with along the way. It's all up to you, your needs, and your creativity.

Astrology Chart

Astrology is the belief that the position of the sun, moon, planets, and stars during a person's birth determines who they are and can predict how their lives will go on any given day. Because of this, an Astrology Chart has several uses. This chart might be helpful if you want to see the personality and ruling element of your future child, your spouse, or even a new professor or boss. You might want to ask which signs, ruling elements, and characteristics you're compatible with. You may also use the dates to see the time frame for when you might meet your potential love match.

Remember, all aspects of one's personality can serve the good in some capacity, so put aside your preconceived notions of what each sign represents. Maintain your neutral posture and be open to any answer.

ARIES (Mar 21 – April 19)
The Element of Fire:
courageous, committed,
passionate, impatient,
short-tempered, aggressive

TAURUS (April 20 – May 20)
The Element of Earth:
reliable, ambitious, practical,
stubborn, uncompromising

GEMINI (May 21 – June 20)
The Element of Air:
affectionate, adaptable,
dynamic, nervous,
passive-aggressive, indecisive

CANCER (June 21 – July 22)
The Element of Water:
emotional, highly
imaginative, intuitive,
timid, manipulative

LEO (July 23 – Aug 22)
The Element of Fire:
bold, warm-hearted,
humorous, good listener,
self-critical, inflexible

VIRGO (Aug 23 – Sep 22)
The Element of Earth:
analytical, kind, practical,
rigid, perfectionist, hardworking

LIBRA (Sep 23 – Oct 22)
The Element of Air:
analytical, diplomatic,
gracious, insecure, flaky,
self-pitying

SCORPIO (Oct 23 – Nov 21)
The Element of Water:
authentic, powerful, brave,
distrustful, emotional,
manipulative

SAGITTARIUS (Nov 22 – Dec 21)
The Element of Fire:
leader, idealistic, humorous,
selfish, impatient, blunt

AQUARIUS (Jan 20 – Feb 18)
The Element of Air:
original, enigmatic,
humanitarian, temperamental

CAPRICORN (Dec 22 – Jan 19)
The Element of Earth:
responsible, disciplined,
family-oriented, unforgiving,
narrow-minded, pessimistic

PISCES (Feb 19 – Mar 20)
The Element of Water:
artistic, observant, gentle,
fearful, overthinker, defensive

For example, you can ask:

Ask

Which astrological sign am I most compatible with?

If you receive multiple answers, narrow it down:

Ask

*Am I more compatible with a Libra
instead of a Taurus?*

Numerical Chart

Numerology is the belief that every number has a unique energy behind it. When constructing your Numerical Chart, it's best to design it so that you are left with the core numbers of numerology, 0–9. This chart can tell you what time you may want to put a plan into action, how many partners you may have in your life, or see how many familiars you might adopt, to name a few examples. You can also use this as a numerology chart to give yourself a daily, or even monthly, forecast.

0 — infinite possibilities, completeness
1 — action, focus
2 — relationship, balance
3 — creativity, fun
4 — structure, discipline

5 — curiosity, adventure

6 — nurture, comfort

7 — spirituality, luck

8 — completeness, success

9 — humanitarian pursuits, intuition

10 — a combination of characteristics 1–9

11 — spiritual mastery, faith

22 — manifestation, logic, and reasoning

33 — altruism, wisdom

When using the chart for numerology, you can ask questions like:

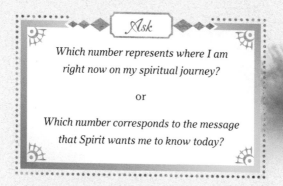

Ask

*Which number represents where I am
right now on my spiritual journey?*

or

*Which number corresponds to the message
that Spirit wants me to know today?*

If you get a combination of numbers, add the single digits
together. For example, 15 turns into $1 + 5 = 6$.

Percentages Chart

A Percentages Chart can be used in many ways, such as how likely you are to get the job, your chances of being asked on a second date, or the likelihood of passing a test. If you need to travel, you can use your pendulum to see the chances of an accident, the level of traffic, how likely it is to rain, or any other obstacle that might interfere with your trip.

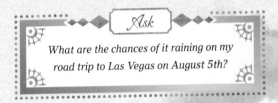

Ask

What are the chances of it raining on my road trip to Las Vegas on August 5th?

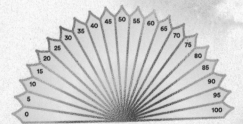

The second usage is how much of something you may need. This can encompass how much money you should put away in savings each week or how much more you need to relax instead of work. You can also see how many more spells you need to incorporate into your day or week. For example:

Ask

What percent of my time should I invest in self-care?

or

What percentage of my day should I spend outdoors?

When designing the chart, you can make it into a circle or semicircle, with each wedge going up in fifths—0%, 5%, 10%, 15%. This way, there's more room for accuracy in your readings.

Compass Chart

A Compass Chart can be helpful for quite a few things. It's perfect for giving succinct directions for finding missing items. You can also use this chart to tell you where to move, which locations to vacation, or help you decide where you might want to go to school. For example, you can ask questions like:

Ask

Should I go to college on the west or east coast?

or

Should I vacation in the south where it's warmer or the north where it's colder?

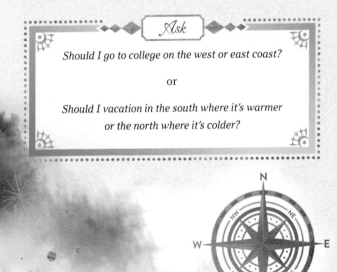

You can also use this chart for elemental magic. Each direction has one of the four elements attached to it and can aid you in the creation of certain spells. The list below shows each direction and the element, season, animal, and magical property associated with it.

EAST – Air
Season: spring
Animal: bee
Property: logic

WEST – Water
Season: autumn
Animal: frog
Property: emotions

NORTH – Earth
Season: winter
Animal: bear
Property: growth

SOUTH – Fire
Season: summer
Animal: snake
Property: purification

Ask

Which directional element should I work with today?

Alphabetical Chart

An Alphabetical Chart looks similar to a Ouija board, but they are *not* the same. The latter requires opening up the spirit world in order to speak to the dead or any other beings that pass through. An Alphabetical Chart with a pendulum calls upon an already-present spirit guide or deity and your subconscious. So, there's no need to be afraid or cautious when using or making this chart.

An Alphabetical Chart can be helpful because it literally spells out the answer. It's very fluid in the sense that you can ask simply for the first letter of the answer to your question, or you can ask for the entire word. When done with practice, this chart can send very specific and clear answers. You can use it to decide which names you might want for your future child or a new pet. Or you can use it to craft a new identity for yourself. In witchcraft, you can give yourself a spiritual name that only you know. There are a plethora of uses owing to its versatile nature.

You can also use this chart to make bigger life decisions, such as where you should move to. Going further, you can use it to decide what country you'd like to visit on your next vacation. Pair this with the Months Chart (see pages 28–29), and you can pick the specific day you should embark. Some example questions are:

Ask

Which letter does my new spirit name start with?

or

The next country I'll visit starts with which letter?

You can construct this chart as either a semicircle or a full circle. Be sure to make its segments wide enough so that you will be able to easily tell which letter is the answer to your question.

Days of the Week Chart

A Days of the Week Chart represents all seven days of the week. Maybe you're curious about which is the best day to meet with a psychic or palm reader. You might wonder when you should set aside time for a spa day. Use your pendulum, and you should get the answer right away.

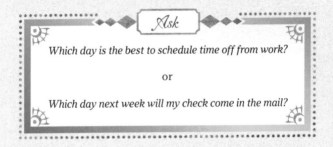

Ask

Which day is the best to schedule time off from work?

or

Which day next week will my check come in the mail?

The secondary usage is to read the days like a horoscope of sorts. Each day has its own deity that has their own characteristics.

SUNDAY: Sun
Properties: prosperity, success, popularity

THURSDAY: Jupiter
Properties: healing, strength, abundance

MONDAY: Moon
Properties: peace, insightfulness, emotion

FRIDAY: Venus
Properties: love, romance, passion

TUESDAY: Mars
Properties: courage, victory, protection

SATURDAY: Saturn
Properties: wisdom, spirituality, cleansing

WEDNESDAY: Mercury
Properties: communication, change, creativity

If you use this interpretation, you can ask what types of qualities you should exhibit today. Or you can inquire about which Ruler will support you. For example, ask:

Ask

Which Ruler's properties do I need to emulate today?

Months Chart

A Months Chart is perfect for witches who don't need to get as specific as a day chart but need to know when, during the course of a year, is the best time for any given event. One example might be when to start a spell that takes several days to complete. Or maybe you're looking to find out when you can expect a financial windfall to happen. Or even yet, you might want to know when you should expect a manifestation to begin to materialize. This chart comes in handy for countless reasons, but a common use is as a general horoscope, utilizing the deities and characteristics of each month according to the Roman gods and goddesses.

JANUARY – Juno
Characteristics: loyalty, marriage, birth

FEBRUARY – Neptune
Characteristics: victory, instability, emotions

MARCH – Minerva
Characteristics: creativity, wisdom, education

APRIL – Venus
Characteristics: love, romance, passion

MAY – Apollo
Characteristics: healing, artistic pursuit, intuition

JUNE – Mercury
Characteristics: economic prosperity, speed, communication

JULY – Jupiter
Characteristics: leadership, logic, spirituality

AUGUST – Ceres
Characteristics: growth, fertility, maternal love

SEPTEMBER – Vulcan
Characteristics: craftsmanship, wild temperament, disadvantage

OCTOBER – Mars
Characteristics: protection, conflict, growth

NOVEMBER – Diana
Characteristics: justice, love for nature, ambition

DECEMBER – Vesta
Characteristics: stability, family, community

Ask

In which month will I meet my soulmate?

or

During which month will my goals manifest?

Phases of the Moon Chart

A full moon cycle takes place each month, with most phases lasting between three and four days. It begins with the Dark Moon, right before the moon begins a new cycle, all the way to the Waxing Crescent phase, when the moon has completed her journey and is on the verge of a new beginning, the New Moon.

Use this chart to narrow down to a specific block of time during the month when something can or should occur. Another great option for spell planning or manifestation, this chart should be used in tandem with your regional moon phase calendar, if you'd like your answer to be even more precise. Pay attention to the properties associated with each phase, as these should be incorporated with your intention when dowsing this chart.

Phase: DARK MOON
Properties: rest, contemplation

Phase: NEW MOON
Properties: new beginnings, unlimited potential

Phase: WAXING CRESCENT
Properties: clarification, hope, dreams

Phase: FIRST QUARTER
Properties: courage to move forward, new adventures, action

Phase: WAXING GIBBOUS
Properties: making changes, hard work, success

Phase: FULL MOON
Properties: manifestation, celebration, fulfillment

Phase: WANING GIBBOUS
Properties: community, sharing abundance, self-care

Phase: LAST QUARTER
Properties: new knowledge, readjustment, transition

Phase: WAXING CRESCENT
Properties: reflection, cleansing, wisdom

If you incorporate the meanings of each phase, you can further contextualize your answers. For example, ask:

Ask

During which moon phase would it be ideal to start [your project]?

or

Which moon phase will be most effective when performing a [love] spell?

If your pendulum swings over the First Quarter phase, it is telling you that this is the right time to take the necessary steps to make your goal come true. If your pendulum swings over the Waxing Crescent phase, it might tell you to reflect on your plans, cleanse your mind of any doubt, and move forward with all you know about your process. In this way, you can use the Moon Chart to gain extra insight into what you need to know.

Ask

During which moon phase this month will my powers of manifestation be strongest?

or

If my schedule is busy during the Dark Moon, during which moon phase should I focus on rest?

Chakra Chart

Think of chakras as strategically placed wheels spinning inside us, letting energy pass through them on to the next chakra point in our bodies. When they are in balance, we are healthy, high-functioning people. But when they're not, we can become sick, despondent, and unhealthy. That's why it's important, especially in witchcraft, to check in with your chakras every day to ensure you're taking care of your spiritual health as well as your physical being.

ROOT CHAKRA – Base of the spine
Color: Red
Function: Controls sense of survival and independence
Blockage: Leads to anxiety and insecurity

SACRAL CHAKRA – Naval
Color: Orange
Function: Controls well-being, pleasure, and sexuality
Blockage: Leads to unnecessary guilt and emotional instability

SOLAR PLEXUS CHAKRA – Center of the torso
Color: Yellow
Function: Controls confidence and self-esteem
Blockage: Leads to procrastination and stagnation

HEART CHAKRA — Heart
Color: Green
Function: Controls love and inner peace
Blockage: Leads to loneliness and codependency

THROAT CHAKRA — Throat
Color: Blue
Function: Controls communication and honesty
Blockage: Leads to the inability to speak your mind

THIRD EYE CHAKRA — Between the eyebrows
Color: Indigo
Function: Controls intuition and wisdom
Blockage: Leads to close-mindedness and mistrust

CROWN CHAKRA — Top of the head
Color: Violet
Function: Controls spiritual life and connection
Blockage: Leads to stubbornness and narrow-mindedness

Ask

Which chakra is currently blocked in my body?

Herbal Chart

Herbs do so much for us that it can be difficult to decide which one to use, especially if you don't have a green thumb, cook often, or use herbs in your spell casting. Thankfully, this chart can help with selecting herbs for a variety of situations. Maybe you want to craft a new spell and you'd like an herb to boost its magic. Or you might want to know which herb you should carry with you throughout your day for luck, love, or protection. On the following chart are common herbs and their ritualistic uses.

ROSEMARY: all-purpose herb to boost energies

BASIL: luck, good fortune, money

CHAMOMILE: sleep, healing, purification

LAVENDER: relaxation, dreams, beauty

CATNIP: sensuality, platonic love, an alternative to white sage

BAY: wishes, enhanced psychic abilities

YARROW: healing, courage, dreamwork

MINT: healing, financial gain

MUGWORT: divination, cleansing

ROSE: love, beauty

STAR ANISE: Dark Moon divination

CINNAMON: amplification of magic, release

THYME: joy, clarity

Write one herb per section on your chart, hover your pendulum, and ask:

Ask

Which herb would best suit my needs today?

Witch's Rune Chart

Typically made by a practicing witch, witch's runes are more personalized than common rune sets, such as Nordic or Celtic runes. Make sure there are twenty-four symbols on your chart (one for each rune). You can refer to the Elder Futhark alphabet (most common) or create your own symbols with personalized meanings (encouraged).

Used as an alternative to casting stones or bones, witch's rune charts can reveal the future, the present, and relationships to the past. You can construct sections of your chart using the following chart for inspiration, or by assigning your own meanings to symbols that are relevant to you.

THE SUN: new beginnings, achievements

THE MOON: emotional issues, mysteries

FLIGHT: travel, communication

RINGS: connection, people coming together

ROMANCE: love, deep commitment

WOMAN: compassion, homemaking, an elder

MAN: action, protection, an elder

HARVEST: fruits of labor, return on investment

CROSSROADS: decision needed, options

THE STAR: inspiration, hope

WAVES: constant change, insecurity

THE SCYTHE: endings, death

THE EYE: truth, clarity

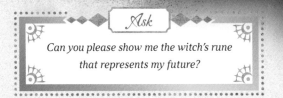

Ask

Can you please show me the witch's rune that represents my future?

1. Write down the answer in a separate notebook. Then ask the same question for the present and past.

2. Once you write everything down, you can intuit your reading based on the results.

Color Chart

While most of us have a favorite color, they each have magical properties associated with them, so when constructing this chart, it's important to give equal credence and space to each color so that your pendulum can choose the answer freely using your energy, but not your influence.

RED: lust and love, warning, rage

PINK: romance, love, kindness

ORANGE: warmth, jubilance, extroversion

YELLOW: inspiration, joy, clarity

GREEN: growth, luck, healing

BLUE: calm, cold, understanding

PURPLE: enigma, royalty, wisdom

BROWN: practicality, earth, grounding

BLACK: the unknown, death, protection

WHITE: purity, spirit, divinity

Maybe you want to paint your walls a new color or you want help deciding which color best represents you. In these cases, you should ask:

Ask

Which color's properties do I need to embody the most right now?

If you want to use colors for divination, be sure to be specific on what you're looking for. You don't want to get a reading based on the here and now when you're looking to examine your past:

Ask

Which color best reflects the state of my past?

If you're getting multiple answers, you may combine the colors to reveal a deeper overall message. For example, red, yellow, and white would suggest you have an angry, unhappy past with a joyous present and a bright future.

Crystal Chart

Accumulating a crystal collection can be costly and take some time, so this chart can work as a stand in as you can amass that collection. Use the following list to construct your chart:

GARNET: passion, verve, returns hexes to sender

ROSE QUARTZ: love, friendship, healing from heartbreak

CARNELIAN: manifesting, courage, motivation

JADE: emotional health, inner peace

BLUE LACE AGATE: peace, tranquility, meditation

TURQUOISE: wisdom, positivity, compassion

AMETHYST: intuition, psychic skills, dispels nightmares

SMOKY QUARTZ: grounding, optimism, overcoming fear

JASPER: determination, stability, balance

TIGER'S EYE: integrity, loyalty, repels negativity

MOONSTONE: emotional connection, moon magic, dreamwork

OBSIDIAN: protection, grounding, mystery

CLEAR QUARTZ: clarity, all purpose, purification

AMBER: vitality, healing, converts negative energy to positive energy

On a circle or semi-circular chart, place the names of the crystals you would use if you had them on hand. Make sure you and your chart have been cleansed and ask questions similar to:

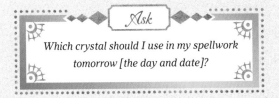

Ask

Which crystal should I use in my spellwork tomorrow [the day and date]?

Self-Affirmation Chart

There are moments when we feel as though our lives are caving in and we aren't fulfilling our potential. Maybe we're falling behind at work or we're not being the best friend, parent, or partner we could be. A Self-Affirmation Chart can be a love letter from the Divine when you're not feeling your best. To find affirmations to place on your chart, you can listen to your intuition to come up with some on your own, or you can refer to the following suggestions.

- I prove every day that I can push through challenges.
- I can and will manifest the life I dream of.
- I am grateful for what I have even if I still want more.
- I am allowed to take a break. I work very hard.
- I am proud of myself for doing the best I can.
- My best isn't always 100%, and that's okay.
- I am on a journey that's uniquely mine.
- I love myself for always trying, even when I don't succeed.

On a circular or semicircular chart, create eight sections and write in affirmations that you think you may need. Hover your pendulum over the chart and ask:

Ask

Which affirmation do I need to hear today?

or

Can you please tell me the truth about myself right now?

2

Making Decisions

NOW THAT YOU'RE FAMILIAR WITH charts and have some of your own, you can use them for improving your outlook and life's circumstances. Charts are a great addition to your arsenal of magic, but they can also be quite limiting because they focus on only one avenue of dowsing answers. When seeking broader answers, you can ask virtually anything as long as the question is phrased to give a "yes," "no," or "maybe."

The most popular use of pendulums is while making decisions and appealing to the Divine for clarity. Life is almost entirely made up of choices—the choices of those who came before us manifested through our behaviors, and the choices we make every day. Because there are so many options given to us, we can easily get overwhelmed and not know which direction we should go. This is why we love pendulum magic! It's always happy to answer you, no matter how insignificant the question might appear on the surface, so don't hold back if you feel called to dowse.

When dowsing in decision making, it's of the utmost importance that you prepare yourself for each session. Remember to always begin by grounding yourself and centering your emotions. When asking questions, we can get emotionally caught up in the answers, which can interfere with how we read them. Clear your mind of wants and expectations and trust the Divine to guide your pendulum to the answers you need to hear. So mote it be.

Which Career Is Right for You?

Our career or livelihood is a major part of our lives, offering personal fulfillment and financial security. Choosing one is a huge life decision that must be taken seriously in order to lead a happy and fulfilling existence. You might be looking to start your life's work, or it might already be established but you feel unsatisfied and underappreciated. In these moments, it's worth looking into another field of work.

Gather:

- ♦ Pendulum
- ♦ Computer for research
- ♦ Pen and paper
- ♦ Envelopes

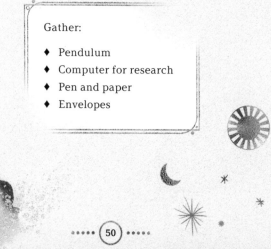

1. Research the fields you're interested in. You'll want a few options. Create a chart with your options and ask:

Ask

Which field is best suited to my talents?

2. Once you know which field to go to, research available positions in your area and apply to them.

3. Once you have two tempting offers, write them down on separate pieces of paper and place them in separate envelopes, shuffling them so you don't know the contents.

4. Set the envelopes side-by-side, then hover your pendulum over them and ask:

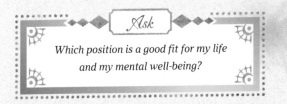

Ask

Which position is a good fit for my life and my mental well-being?

5. When it indicates one envelope more strongly than the other, open the envelope and read your answer.

Investment Decisions

When investing in the stock market, start by giving yourself foundational knowledge by researching such topics as stocks and bonds, 401K savings, retirement accounts, earnings per share, and historical returns. From here, look into individual companies you'd like to invest in. You can take the suggestions of a broker, or you can choose stocks based on companies you think (or your intuition is telling you) will grow in value.

Gather:

♦ Green aventurine pendulum for money
♦ Yes/No Chart (optional)

1. Make a list of companies you'd like to invest in.

2. Hover your pendulum over your Yes/No Chart or your palm, and as you say each company name, ask:

Ask

Will it benefit me to add this company to my stock portfolio?

3. Then, once you're ready to diversify your portfolio, look into more secure options for investment:

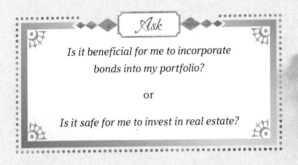

Ask

Is it beneficial for me to incorporate bonds into my portfolio?

or

Is it safe for me to invest in real estate?

Investing doesn't have to be difficult, especially if you have your pendulum to guide you through it.

Budgeting Decisions

Making and sticking to a budget can be challenging. There are times when we have planned our spending out, but a surprise expense may arise and muddy the waters. That's the magic of budgeting. You can put away money for surprises—if you can afford to. The question then is what to do with the disposable income you have left after all the necessities have been paid for. How much should you put in savings? Can you afford to meet friends for happy hour? Or will you need that money down the line? What about splurging? With some time and extra thinking, you can solve your budgeting problems.

Gather:

♦ Pendulum
♦ Computer
♦ Notebook or sheet of paper (optional)
♦ Yes/No Chart (optional)

1. Tally up your bills and crucial expenses and subtract that total from your monthly pay.

2. What is left is used for play, but it's smart to put some away for emergencies. Ask your pendulum:

Ask

Will it be sustainable in the long run to put away [$30] per week instead of [$50]?

3. You can also write out your spending categories and dowse over each one or use your palm or Yes/No Chart as an alternative.

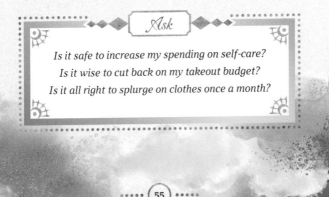

Ask

Is it safe to increase my spending on self-care?

Is it wise to cut back on my takeout budget?

Is it all right to splurge on clothes once a month?

Buying a Car

A car is a huge investment for anyone. There are the initial costs, maintenance, insurance, and government fees that need to be considered. When you're ready to make the purchase, your pendulum can help.

Gather:

♦ Pendulum
♦ Computer and printer
♦ Pen and paper
♦ Yes/No Chart (optional)

1. Do some research before consulting your pendulum. Think about whether you want a new or used car, gas mileage, size, then make and model. Narrow your search down to two or three cars and write down or print out pictures of each car.

2. Hover your pendulum over your options and ask:

> *Ask*
>
> *Which one is the right car for me?*

3. Go out and test drive the car and gather the financial information for it.

4. Using either a Yes/No Chart or your palm, ask:

> *Ask*
>
> *Is this car financially sustainable for me?*

Once you have your answers, travel forth in safety and style. So mote it be.

Finding Your Dwelling

Your dwelling is your sanctuary, the one place where you can always be your authentic self. There are so many factors in deciding where you'll call home. You need to consider whether you'll rent or buy, how much space you'll need, if pets are allowed, or whether you'll have a roommate.

Gather:

♦ Pendulum
♦ Computer
♦ Pen and paper
♦ Any legal paperwork involved

1. Begin your search by looking into which properties are in your price range. From there, call each real estate agent to see if the property is still available and tour the spaces.

2. Before going, write down the address of each property and a list of questions—included amenities, lease agreement, and anything else that's relevant to you.

3. This step is a sort of choose-your-own-adventure: You can create a chart with your property options and dowse your questions, or you can take your pendulum with you while touring properties and dowse the space directly. Once you decide your course of action, hover your pendulum and ask the following questions, paying close attention to the strength of each answer:

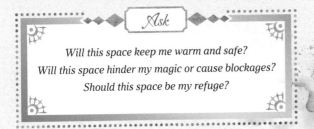

Ask

Will this space keep me warm and safe?
Will this space hinder my magic or cause blockages?
Should this space be my refuge?

4. When you have your answers, secure the place as soon as possible by submitting the legal paperwork.

Painting Your Dwelling

Our homes are an expression of who we are and what we allow in our spaces. This is why the most important part of having an abode is choosing the decorations, furniture, and colors.

Many of us don't realize how strongly colors affect us. Have you ever been in a dreary building with no pictures or paintings and a bland color on the walls? Those places tend to bring down our mood and restrict our creative expression. Because we spend much of our time at home, it is vital to our practice and overall well-being to pick colors that will bring us joy and contentment. When performing this spell, be mindful of your preferences but try not to influence your pendulum's answers.

Gather:

♦ Pendulum
♦ Color palette(s)
♦ Color Chart (optional)

1. Before you begin, hold your hands over the palette and Color Chart (if using). This will help the right color connect to you. Take three deep breaths and adjust your stance to be stable and grounded. Imagine infusing your energy into the colors. Hover your pendulum over each hue and ask:

Ask

Will this color bring joy to my home?

2. You can get more specific with your questions, like asking about the color of the outside of the house or, if you'd like, each individual room. Be as specific as possible to get the right result. If your pendulum picks multiple colors and you just want one, ask:

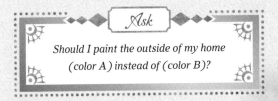

Ask

Should I paint the outside of my home
(color A) instead of (color B)?

3. From here, you can even choose which paint company you should buy from to ensure total harmony.

Appliances for Your Dwelling

At some point in your life, you're going to have to buy a new appliance for your dwelling. Whether you're moving into a new space or need to replace an older machine, it's unavoidable. Because appliances can be pricey, there are many methods to getting one. You can buy from the thrift store, at yard sales, on resale websites, or from your local appliance store. You can also go for newer, shinier models or less flashy but more practical and less expensive models. As you wade your way through all these options, your pendulum will guide you to the perfect machine for you.

Gather:

♦ Pendulum
♦ Pen and paper
♦ Yes/No Chart (optional)

1. Determine which and how many appliances you need. A new fridge? Microwave? Washer and dryer? Write them down.

2. Look at your budget, which will determine where you buy your appliances from. Make a list of the places you'd like to do your shopping.

3. Go to those places (bring your pendulum) and get a feel for each appliance. Dowse over every machine that feels right to you and ask:

Ask

Is this appliance a good investment for my home?
Will this appliance be a good fit in my space?

4. Don't make any rash decisions. If you must, go home and think it over.

5. Write down each appliance that you're considering buying along with the place you found it.

6. With your remaining options, use your palm or Yes/No Chart and repeat the questions above.

7. Once you have your answer, buy the appliance and enjoy!

Finding Your Future Partner

It's important to know what you want and need in a relationship, especially if you want something long-term. Dating can be time consuming and difficult when there are so many people out there and several others who simply aren't compatible with you. If you don't know what you want out of a significant other, you may be wasting your time with people who aren't right for you.

Whether you've never been in a relationship or you're a serial monogamist, you can benefit from laying everything out on the table to clearly see what you're looking for. Use your pendulum to go over several qualities and see who makes up your ideal future partner. Here are some ideas to get you started:

- Adventurous, brave, creative
- Down-to-earth, energetic, faithful
- Grounded, intelligent, kind
- Loving, optimistic, patient
- Quiet, responsible, tender

Gather:

♦ Rose quartz pendulum for potential love
♦ Pen and paper
♦ Yes/No Chart (optional)
♦ Astrology Chart (optional)

1. Write down the characteristics you're attracted to. Write down as many as you can think of.

2. Hover your pendulum over each characteristic, your palm, or a Yes/No Chart and ask:

Ask

Is this a good quality in my future partner?

3. Go one by one and mark the characteristics your pendulum approved of. After exhausting your list, you can consult the Astrology Chart to narrow down your match.

4. When your list is complete, place it somewhere you will see it before going on any new dates. Don't settle for less.

Confessing to Your Crush

There's nothing quite like having a crush: the thump of your heart when they're near, the warm feeling when they smile at you, and the inability to stop thinking of them. It's one of the best forms of magic. The longer the infatuation goes on, the more it can feel like you're going to burst with overwhelming emotion, like you're stuck in love limbo. Your pendulum can help you determine whether you should confess to your crush or just let your puppy love run its course.

Gather:

- ♦ Rose quartz pendulum for love and affection
- ♦ Meditative music
- ♦ Yes/No Chart (optional)
- ♦ Days of the Week Chart

1. Turn on the meditative music, close your eyes, and take four deep breaths. Because you're invested in the outcome, you need to take this time to relax and calm your heart.

2. Now picture your crush's name in your mind's eye. This will prevent you from getting distracted by their looks and keep you focused on them as a person. With your pendulum and your Yes/No Chart or palm, ask:

Ask

Should I confess my feelings to my crush?

3. If you receive a yes, consult the Days of the Week Chart to pick which day in the upcoming week you should confess.

Ask

On which day this week should I confess my feelings?

When you get your answer, try not to overthink it. Prepare yourself to tell them how you feel. Jump in and be brave!

Should I Stay or Should I Go?

There are moments in a relationship—whether romantic, platonic, or professional—when we are at a crossroads. You may be unhappy in the relationship, but you have a history you're not sure you want to sever. Thankfully, your pendulum can help you decide what you should do for your benefit and, ultimately, the benefit of others.

Gather:

♦ Pendulum
♦ Pen and paper
♦ Computer and printer (optional)
♦ Yes/No Chart (optional)

1. Inscribe the name of the other person in your relationship. If you like, you can print out a picture of them.

2. Take four deep breaths and clear your mind of any lingering emotions.

3. After confirming your answers, hang your pendulum over the person's name or your Yes/No Chart and ask:

Ask

Should I continue my relationship with [name]?

4. If your pendulum says, "unknown," you may ask follow-up questions like:

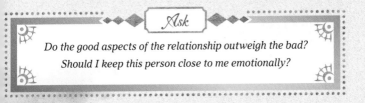

Ask

Do the good aspects of the relationship outweigh the bad?
Should I keep this person close to me emotionally?

5. If your pendulum says to ultimately keep this person in your life, then know that you still have more to teach each other.

When and Where to Vacation

Life is short and it's best to enjoy what you can, while you can. Because of our busy schedules, it can be difficult to make time to enjoy ourselves, but we *must*. Going on vacation improves your mental health, boosts happiness, decreases burnout, and fortifies relationships.

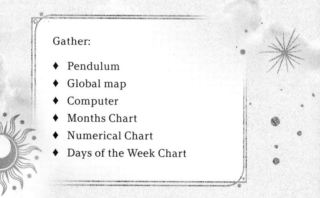

Gather:

♦ Pendulum
♦ Global map
♦ Computer
♦ Months Chart
♦ Numerical Chart
♦ Days of the Week Chart

1. Spread out the global map on a clean surface or download a digital one on a larger screen than your phone.

2. Dowse over each continent until you find the correct country or state to visit.

3. Once you find the right place, research fun things you can do at your chosen location to get you excited.

4. Next, dowse over your Months Chart to decide which is the right month for your trip. If you'd like to ensure good weather, you can divide your Months Chart into three-month blocks to separate out the seasons, then dowse over the block of months you'd like to travel, allowing your pendulum to narrow down to one month.

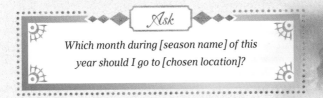

Ask

Which month during [season name] of this year should I go to [chosen location]?

5. From there, dowse over the Numerical Chart to determine how many days you should be away.

6. Use the Days of the Week Chart and determine which day of the week you should start the vacation.

7. Make your plans—and enjoy yourself once you're away!

Where to Volunteer

Giving your time to a cause or institution is a wonderful thing to do. One aspect of witchery means being a part of a bigger community. We simply do better when we're helping other people. Volunteering can provide a sense of purpose, build your community, improve your self-esteem, and increase your social skills. You might be in a position to give your time and skills to a cause, but you don't know what that cause may be. Dowsing is an excellent way to get started.

Gather:

♦ Pendulum
♦ Pen and paper
♦ Yes/No Chart (optional)

1. List your passions. Are civil rights important to you? Do you value education? If you're passionate about a certain area, you're more likely to sustain this commitment.

2. See if your passions intertwine. For example, if you love teaching kids and the outdoors, you could volunteer at a summer camp. If any of your interests do align, this can narrow your search down to something that fulfills you on multiple levels.

3. Search your local area for places to donate your time to. Hopefully they're nearby, and if they aren't, see if you can do virtual work.

4. Now that you know what's out there, write down which causes you most want to give your time. Come up with two or three organizations. Hover your pendulum over each cause, your palm, or your Yes/No Chart and ask:

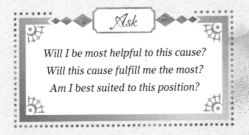

Ask

Will I be most helpful to this cause?
Will this cause fulfill me the most?
Am I best suited to this position?

5. Once you've made the choice, reach out to that organization, and get out of your comfort zone, knowing you'll be making a difference. So mote it be.

Finding a New Hobby

Hobbies are activities done for pleasure in one's free time. Depending on your work and family schedule, along with volunteering, you might not have too much time left over for yourself. But having a hobby is an excellent stress reliever, a road to self-discovery, and a way to be spiritually refreshed. It's a reminder to take time for yourself and enrich your soul.

Gather:

◆ Pendulum
◆ Pen and paper
◆ Representations of the hobby (optional)

1. List your interests. This can be as broad as "learning languages" or as specific as "acrylic nail art." Write down every activity that makes you feel light, fulfilled, or happy. Include your guilty pleasures if you'd like.

2. Narrow down the list to what you want to spend at least 30 minutes a day doing. At this stage, you can pick what you want to expand on.

3. From there, you can either have representations of your prospective hobbies or you can write them down on paper. Dowse over each of them and ask:

Ask

Is this the hobby I should give my time to every day?
Is this hobby the most enriching for me to pursue?

4. Your pendulum will pick up on your subconscious and what you truly want to do. When you single out the preferred hobby, go full force into it. Pursue what makes you happy and what will ultimately better you.

Choosing a Pet

The bond between animals and humans is unlike any other, and nurturing a furry, feathered, or amphibious friend can bring great comfort and joy to your life. So, if you want to add a precious living being to your household, it's important to know which one you want, if they would be a good addition to your life, and if you would be a good caretaker.

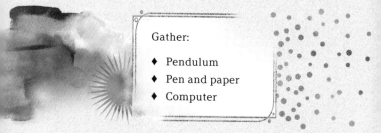

Gather:

♦ Pendulum
♦ Pen and paper
♦ Computer

1. Determine which kinds of pets you can reasonably take care of. Don't bring in an exotic animal if you aren't able to provide the appropriate amount of room or pay for their care or veterinary fees.

2. Out of those animals, list the ones that would best match your needs. Do you want a pet that mostly takes care of itself? Do you want a pet you can nurture? Would you prefer a more energetic pet or a quiet pet?

3. Next, determine where you will get this animal from: a shelter, a breeder, or a pet store? There are many options so choose what feels right for you and your lifestyle.

4. Write down your pet options in a list, then hover your pendulum over each entry and ask,

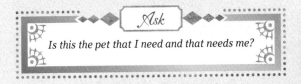

Ask

Is this the pet that I need and that needs me?

5. Grab your pendulum and go meet the pet in person. It might be love at first sight, or you may be conflicted between two or more future companions. Ask one or both of the following questions while hovering your pendulum.

Ask

Is this my new friend?

Is [pet A] a better fit for me than [pet B]?

6. Once you make your choice, bring home your new buddy and delight in the joy and comfort you will bring to each other.

What to Wear
for a Special Occasion

For masculine-presenting people, a sharp suit can fit virtually any special occasion. But femme-presenting people typically have a wider variety of styles to choose from, which also means there are more rules around wardrobe. Sometimes it can be difficult to choose what to wear because you want to look and feel good, but you also need to be socially appropriate. Thankfully, colors have their own magic and can influence how we look and feel, and your pendulum can lead you to presenting your best self.

Gather:

♦ Pendulum
♦ 3 outfits
♦ Color Chart (optional)

1. Consider the event you are attending because that will help narrow down what you should wear. For example, if you're going to a wedding, the rule is to never upstage the bride, so you don't wear white.

2. Next, choose the color(s) that will reflect how you want to feel and what you want to project to others.

3. From there, choose three outfits that fit your criteria. Hover your pendulum over each outfit and ask:

Ask

Is this outfit the best choice for [the event]?

4. If your pendulum says "yes" or "maybe" for two outfits, ask:

Ask

Does [outfit A] project more confidence than [outfit B]?

Does [outfit A] better express who I am than [outfit C]?

5. Now wear your chosen getup and know you look amazing!

Go forth and be fabulous. So mote it be.

Choosing a Houseplant

Adding a new plant to your home is akin to bringing a new life into your space. There are so many benefits to having at least one. They are said to improve air quality, reduce stress, make our minds sharper, and can be therapeutic. We are meant to be around nature, and having plants sharing our space can be our way to connect with the outside world, without the bugs or the allergies.

Gather:

♦ Pendulum
♦ Computer (optional)
♦ Future plants or representations

1. Bring your pendulum to a local nursery or print and lay out images of the plants you're attracted to. The benefit of going directly to the florist is that your pendulum can react more strongly to the energies of each plant, and you can discuss on site with the botanist which plants are best for indoor planting and care instructions; but printing out options works well too.

2. Use your pendulum to dowse over each plant you're interested in, either in person or with your representations. It's possible that your pendulum will choose a couple of options, as the Divine loves all living things. Pay attention to the strength of the swing during the affirmative answers and ask:

Ask

Will this plant be a good addition to my home?

3. If your pendulum says yes to more than one plant, ask if you should get both, or choose the one that had the strongest answer.

Now, go flex that green thumb!

3

Making Discoveries

PENDULUMS ARE WONDERFUL FOR helping us make decisions. Their direct answers can really cut through any confusion and lead us in the right direction. But their power doesn't end there. They can also help us discover the unknown, whether that be a missing person or your life's purpose. A pendulum is a powerful tool that can help you make discoveries about the world around you and what you can accomplish in it. Life is made of discoveries: the good, the bad, the confusing, and the hopeful.

This chapter uncovers the practical, from finding a roommate to more spiritually focused searches, like discovering your patron deity. Because of the subject matter, make sure you're level-headed when dowsing. It's easy to get caught up in your feelings when your future is on the line, but it's important to stay calm while dowsing. Always ask if now is the right time to dowse. If your pendulum says yes, move forward and let the unknown unfold. Seek and you shall find. So mote it be.

Finding a Lost Person

In today's world, we are in constant communication with one another, so when someone goes radio silent, alarm bells go off. Of course, they might simply want to unplug, but if you feel something is off, contact them directly first. Then, reach out to their inner circle. If they still don't turn up, contact the authorities.

Gather:

♦ Pendulum
♦ Map of where the person lives
♦ Compass
♦ Photograph of the person, an item of their clothing, or a sentimental object (optional)
♦ Regional map (optional)

1. Take five slow, deep breaths and imagine what they look like, their mannerisms, and their special features.

2. Find, download, or draw a local map of where the person lives and while hovering your pendulum over each area ask:

Ask

Was [person's name] last seen here?

3. Once you have a positive answer, go to the location, bringing your pendulum with you.

4. Once there, do a breathing exercise to ground yourself in the location and remain calm. Use your compass to face north, then ask:

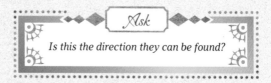

Ask

Is this the direction they can be found?

5. Do this for each direction—north, south, east, and west. When you receive the positive answer, walk in that direction. A stronger swing as you go along will confirm that you're on the right track. Keep going.

6. Once you arrive at the location, look around carefully, calling the person's name until you hear or see them.

7. If this doesn't work, go back home and lay out an item of theirs: a photo, clothing, or sentimental object.

8. Lay out your regional map near your item(s) and dowse over it asking:

Ask

Is this the area where we should look for [person's name]?

9. Once you have narrowed down a region, repeat this process in smaller and smaller areas until you have a specific spot to look for them.

Go and find your loved one safe and sound. So mote it be.

Finding a Lost Pet

Searching for a lost pet can be extra disheartening because pets can't communicate verbally with us. We can't contact them, and depending on what they look like, they might easily blend into their environment. Rely on your pendulum to do the talking. The process is similar to finding a person, but you'll need to get a little more resourceful.

Gather:

- Pendulum
- Item associated with your pet
- Compass

1. Ask your pendulum if your pet wants to be found. This might feel strange because of course you want to find your pet. But if your pet doesn't want to be found, your search might be in vain.

2. If the answer is yes, hold on to the association item and concentrate on their image. You can even think about how much you love their personality—whatever links you to them.

3. If you know your pet was last seen at your house, stand outside your door and use your compass to find north. Do this for each direction—north, south, east, and west—while asking:

Ask

Is this the right direction to go to find [pet's name]?

4. Your pendulum will confirm where to proceed, so follow its lead while calling out your pet's name. Animals can fit into nooks and crannies that people can't, so make sure to check all spaces, even down to your car and yard.

5. When you're nearby, the pendulum will move much more strongly, indicating they're close.

6. If your pet was lost at the park, or in an area you're unfamiliar with, perform this dowsing spell wherever you think they might be lost.

Finding a Lost Object

A bane of human existence is misplacing simple objects. One minute, the remote is in your hand; the next, it's nowhere to be found. You come home with keys in hand, and the next time you need to leave the house, you can't find them. Just like finding living beings, a pendulum can lead you straight to your missing object.

1. You're probably frustrated and annoyed, so begin by grounding yourself with a meditation or breathing exercise.

2. From the center of your home, dangle your pendulum and face each direction outward until you receive a positive answer.

3. Once you have the right direction, begin to slowly walk, being careful to be very steady of hand. When the pendulum swings the hardest, you're getting close! The question you ask is determined by your environment, so for example, ask something like:

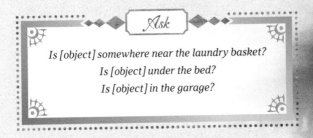

Ask

Is [object] somewhere near the laundry basket?

Is [object] under the bed?

Is [object] in the garage?

4. If yes, ask your pendulum to lead you to the exact spot.

Finding Your Divinity

We are all divine creatures, whether we always feel like it or not. We are bombarded with constant societal messaging that we are not thin enough, successful enough, popular enough, and so on. But we know where we come from and who we are—it's time we go back to it. You may have misplaced your divinity, but you can always find it again.

Gather:

♦ Pendulum

♦ 1 purple candle to represent your inner self

♦ Pen and paper

1. Before you begin, place your candle in a cleansed space so that you are bathed in its light.

2. Inscribe some positive affirmations on the paper. You may jot down phrases like, *I am one with the Universe, I am divine,* or *I am special as I am;* or refer to the list of affirmations on page 44.

3. Inscribe as many affirmations as you can think of and narrow them down to about two or three.

4. Hover your pendulum over one phrase. Say it aloud and see if the pendulum agrees with you. If you get a no, move to the next phrase and repeat the steps above.

5. If you still get a no, this means you do not believe what you are saying, so ask your pendulum what you can do to change that. Use yes-or-no questions until you get the insight you need. Ask:

Ask

Do I have any chakra blockages?
Should I perform a ritual for Spirit?

6. Once you have your answer, do as the pendulum asks, then repeat this spell until you have reawakened the light within.

Finding a Soul Mate

Everyone wants to find a soul mate—the person who's supposed to be *the one* for you. Some believe that anyone can be your soulmate and others hold the idea that your soulmate is one specific person and they alone are destined to be with you. Either way, it's time to take the first step. For this spell, keep an impartial heart and try not to influence the pendulum, otherwise it might lead you astray.

Gather:

♦ Rose quartz pendulum for love
♦ Incense for cleansing
♦ Pen and paper
♦ Yes/No Chart (optional)

1. Light the incense and let it permeate the entire space, keeping a window cracked. Pass your pendulum through the smoke several times.

2. Arrange your workspace so that it's clear of any clutter. Say aloud this affirmation: *I am looking for my soul mate, someone who will love me for who I am and support me.*

3. Write down any questions you have, including:

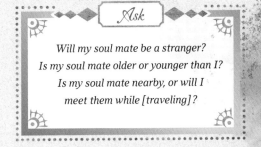

Ask

Will my soul mate be a stranger?
Is my soul mate older or younger than I?
Is my soul mate nearby, or will I meet them while [traveling]?

4. Next, hold your pendulum in your hand and allow your intention to funnel into it. Remember to stay calm and objective. If you feel your heart race, take four deep breaths. Then, bring your presence back to the room.

5. Hover your pendulum over each question, your palm, or your Yes/No Chart and ask away! Be sure to remember or write down your answers.

Finding Your Purpose

Having a *purpose* is the idea that we were put on this earth to do a specific, special thing; something that's meant to fulfill us and give us focus and direction in our lives. To have a purpose in this ever-changing, ever-evolving life helps us grow as we adopt new skills and learn fresh lessons to help us reach for our Higher Selves. Today, with your pendulum, you will find a purpose that you can cling to.

Gather:

♦ Pendulum

♦ Pen and paper

♦ Yes/No Chart (optional)

1. Establish what you love to do. Write down all the activities you enjoy. Space them out on the paper.

2. With your pendulum, ask:

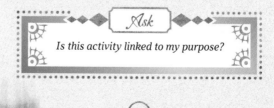

Ask

Is this activity linked to my purpose?

3. Watch the answers. If the pendulum chooses two or more activities, ask:

Is [activity A] better linked to my purpose than [activity B]?

Is [activity A] better suited to my purpose than [activity C]?

4. From there, if your pendulum has still picked more than one activity, consider that maybe your purpose includes two aspects.

5. If so, you can put the pieces together to come up with a unique situation. The more niche, the more direct the answer.

6. When you've narrowed your options down to one, use your palm or your Yes/No Chart to ask the final question:

Is this my purpose?

7. If the answer is no, repeat the steps with new ideas until you get a positive answer.

What's Holding You Back?

The past makes up who and what we are in the present, but it can, if we let it, control our future. If you feel as though you're stuck in the past, you can use your pendulum to discover what is inhibiting you from living your best life.

Gather:

♦ Pendulum
♦ Pen and paper
♦ Yes/No Chart (optional)

1. Sitting in a comfortable position, write down major moments in your past. How have these affected your relationships, your outlook, your current situation?

2. Write down on a separate paper what you can't let go of, for example, family, friends, or romantic relationships. Hover your pendulum over your palm or Yes/No Chart and ask:

Ask

Is this aspect of my past holding me back now?

3. From there, get more specific:

Is my relationship with my [family member] holding me back?

Is my breakup with [ex's name] interfering with my present life?

4. Once you have your answers, ask:

Should I forgive [family member]?

Should I cut them out of my life?

5. Keep asking until you find the answers you need.

6. Cutting cords can be difficult so consider consulting a counselor or therapist for further insight.

Why Are You Suffering?

If left unchecked, negative emotions can snowball into a deep sense of dissatisfaction. This occurs when we're not in tune with our inner lives and are solely focused on external factors. When this happens, it can be difficult to decipher what's the root cause of our suffering. But with some time and your pendulum, you can find the answers you seek.

Gather:

♦ Shungite stone pendulum to promote overall healing
♦ Pen and paper
♦ Meditative music

1. Write down the words "mentally," "spiritually," and "emotionally" on a piece of paper. Then ask:

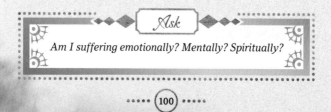

Ask

Am I suffering emotionally? Mentally? Spiritually?

2. When you get a positive answer, use your pendulum to narrow down why specifically you are suffering in this area. Here, you'll need to do some soul searching. Play the meditative music and get comfortable.

3. Close your eyes and take four long, even breaths. Breathe in complete focus and calm; breathe out any distractions or nerves. Ask:

Ask

Do I need to release something or someone energetically?

4. Keep asking more questions and get as specific as possible.

5. When you get to the answer, take it to a psychiatric professional or counselor to help you heal from this burden.

Discovering Hidden Truth

Insecurities, misconceptions, and internalized criticism impede our self-discovery. For this spell, use the Astrology Chart to give some more insight into which personality characteristics might be waning in your life. Knowing what you need to embody to be whole can reveal who you are deeper down. Use this spell throughout your life to maintain your self-discovery.

Gather:

♦ Pendulum
♦ Pen and paper
♦ Astrology Chart

1. Clear your space and place your Astrology Chart before you. Say aloud, *I want to discover myself.* Then, ask your first question:

Ask

Which sign's characteristics am I most in need of emulating now?

2. List all the characteristics that belong to the sign your pendulum chose, discarding qualities that you know through intuition you don't need.

3. Hover your pendulum over each entry on the list and ask:

Ask

Will embodying [characteristic] bring me to a deeper truth?

4. Write your final characteristics and place the list somewhere you can see it daily—the bathroom mirror, taped to the coffee pot, next to your bed. Bring your awareness to the list throughout your day and watch how your inner truths will be revealed as time passes.

Discovering Your Deity

Rather than following an organized religion, many have instead looked for their own patron deity—a divine being that a person feels most connected with or who embodies their own beliefs. In this spell, you'll discover which qualities you most admire to determine who will be your patron deity.

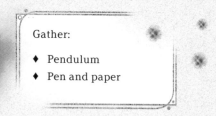

Gather:

♦ Pendulum
♦ Pen and paper

1. Without self-editing, write down what values and forces you believe in. This can mean justice, war, love, the power of the domestic, or any others important to you.

2. Use your pendulum on each characteristic, one by one, and ask:

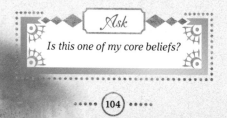

Ask

Is this one of my core beliefs?

3. Record what the pendulum says until you've narrowed it down to about five characteristics.

4. Put your tools away and research which deities match those characteristics.

5. If you find one that matches, congrats! If not, narrow it down further to two or three divine beings.

6. Write down the names of the deities. Dowse over each name and ask:

Ask

Is [name of god/goddess] my patron deity?

7. Note that you can have more than one patron deity, but to begin, try to focus on one. Enjoy getting to know them.

Finding Harmony in Your Home

Feng shui, an Eastern philosophy, is the practice of arranging the pieces in living spaces in such a way that they create balance. It's meant to allow the energy to flow easily in your home from one space to the next. With some time, muscle, and your pendulum, you can create the space you want.

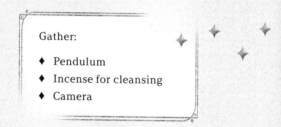

Gather:

♦ Pendulum
♦ Incense for cleansing
♦ Camera

1. Walk through the most traveled path in your living room carrying the incense to cleanse the room.

2. Take pictures of each room, focusing on the furniture arrangements and decor. This is for later reference. If you have a large space, focus on the rooms you use most.

3. From there, dowse every space with your pendulum while asking:

Ask

Is the energy in this room positive?

4. If you get a negative answer, follow up with a specific question like,

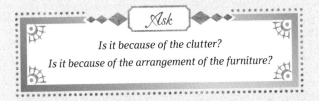

Ask

Is it because of the clutter?

Is it because of the arrangement of the furniture?

5. When you have your answers, refer to the pictures to get a better idea of what can be moved and how each room looks. Actively make some changes.

Finding the Right Roommate

You may be living on your own and need help making the rent, or you may want to open your home to share with other people. It's important to know that the person (or people) you're going to live with is compatible with you.

Gather:

♦ Pendulum
♦ Pen and paper

1. When inviting people to your home, do your research before allowing anyone in. If you find someone you're comfortable meeting, ask your pendulum:

Ask

Will I be safe if I invite this person to my home?

2. If you get a positive answer, initiate the meeting. You can even talk over the phone first to get a sense of who the person is.

3. When the meeting is over, take note of the person you met. Include their name and what vibes you get from them. If at any point you feel uncomfortable, *do not* ignore that feeling. Hover your pendulum over your notes and ask:

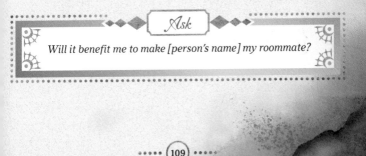

Ask

Will it benefit me to make [person's name] my roommate?

Are They a Match?

Playing matchmaker can be tricky—you might be invested in the result, skewing the answer, or you might be told about a match that the other person might not feel ready to hear. If you're able to remain calm and others are receptive, your pendulum can give you insight into whether or not you've got a love match right in front of you.

Gather:

♦ Rose quartz pendulum for love
♦ Incense
♦ Meditative music
♦ Pen and paper

1. Use the incense to cleanse the space, then play the meditative music to set the scene.

2. Take a deep breath and give yourself 10 minutes to settle and clear your mind. The thing you most want to avoid is projecting your feelings onto the answer.

3. When you're clear-headed, write down the names of the two people on separate pieces of paper and put the papers next to each other. Leave space for the pendulum to hang in between them. Ask:

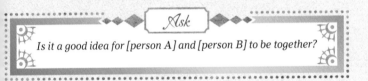

Ask

Is it a good idea for [person A] and [person B] to be together?

4. If you get a positive answer, do not try to force the new pairing, aside from making an introduction. If these people are meant to be a good match, it will happen organically.

5. If you get a negative answer, don't take it as a sign to ask about other possible relationships to fill the gap. It's okay to be single.

Finding EMFs

EMF stands for electromagnetic frequencies, a type of radiation. Though that sounds a bit scary, most of the EMFs we're exposed to are low-level, nonionizing radiation, meaning they won't harm us. However, just because they're harmless, it doesn't mean they don't affect us. Some side effects of exposure to EMFs for long periods are headaches, dizziness, difficulty concentrating, and sleep problems. Because most of the time we're around electronics that emit radiation, it can be difficult to tell which device is causing problems. Thankfully, with your pendulum, you can find the source.

Gather:

♦ Crystal pendulum
♦ Salt or incense
♦ Electronics you interact with daily
   (cellphone, laptop, Wi-Fi router)

1. First, cleanse your pendulum by either allowing it to sit in salt overnight or passing it through incense smoke.

2. State your intentions out loud: *I want to see which EMF device is affecting my health.*

3. Next, ask your pendulum:

Ask

Which direction will you swing during this spell?

4. This will determine how your pendulum will show you how much radiation is coming from each device. Face north.

5. Hang your pendulum over the devices you suspect may be affecting your health.

6. See how wildly it swings and use this to determine which device is the main culprit.

7. When you have the answer, limit your usage. You can even carry shungite with you or place it around the offender to protect you from EMF effects.

Are You Unlucky?

Luck is an elusive force that takes many forms. There are deities, crystals, and tarot cards dedicated to it. Luck is defined as a force that brings good fortune to or adversity against an individual. Everyone wants to be lucky, but not all of us have chance on our side. Use this spell to discover whether or not you're unlucky, and if you are, what you can do to enhance your luck. A wood pendulum is preferable because it won't emit its own frequencies.

Gather:

- Non-crystal pendulum
- Yes/No Chart (optional)
- Jade for luck
- Basil for luck
- Personal lucky charms

1. Hover your (preferably wood) pendulum that won't emit its own frequencies over your palm or a Yes/No Chart and ask:

> *Ask*
>
> *Am I unlucky?*

If you get a negative response, stop here. If you get a positive answer, pray to Spirit by saying aloud, *Spirit, grant me the power of luck as I change my fortune.*

2. Lay the jade out, hover your pendulum over it, your palm, or your Yes/No Chart and ask:

Ask

Is this what I need to turn my luck around?

3. If yes, keep the jade in your pocket. If no, then add the basil to the jade and ask the question again. If you continue to get a negative answer, add a lucky charm one by one until you receive a yes.

4. Place all items in a sachet and keep it on or near you.

Discovering Divination Tools

Although a pendulum is an excellent tool for dowsing and divining, there are other mystical tools that can be wonderful additions for any witch or practitioner. Some methods include tarot cards, reading tea leaves, crystal balls, scrying mirrors, pulling runes, dice, or colored ribbons; all of which will enhance your connection with the Divine. Use your pendulum to determine which tool will be the best companion for your pendulum work.

Gather:

♦ Pendulum

♦ Computer

♦ Pen and paper

♦ DIY Chart (optional)

1. Research methods of divination and make a list of the ones that interest you.

2. When you have a reasonably long list, write down each method on a piece of paper or choose a DIY Chart (pages 11–15).

3. Take four calming breaths, hover your pendulum over the chart or list and ask:

Ask

Which divination method is the right one for me?

4. If you get multiple tugs, ask:

Ask

Is [method A] a better fit for me than [method B]?

5. Once you have your answer, dive into research and improve your craft. Don't forget to practice, practice, practice!

Discovering New Music

Music is essential to our well-being as it can help lower anxiety, improve brain function, and manage pain. Music can take you back to a years-old memory, lift your mood, and add pleasure to your life. Because music carries so much meaning for us, we may get stuck in our genres without listening to something new. If you're a little bored with your current selection, or it longer speaks to you, use your pendulum to find a new musical joy.

Gather:

♦ Pendulum
♦ Computer
♦ Pen and paper

1. There are many genres and subgenres of music that you may not be aware of. To start, research and list all the genres you aren't familiar with on a piece of paper.

2. Dowse over each one and ask:

Ask

Should I look into this genre of music?

3. If your pendulum says yes to multiple genres, pick the one out of the bunch that interests you the most.

4. From there, you can look into the subgenres that may not be as mainstream. For example, if your pendulum picks electronic music, you can write down "synthwave," and from there you can go into "outrun," "dreamwave," and more.

5. Get as in-depth as you want until you're satisfied. Then go explore some new tunes!

6. Once you have new music, put it on and (this is the most important part) have a personal dance party! Dance however your body wants to move, allow yourself to get swept away. Fall in love with the music.

4

Eclectic
Magic

As we've seen, pendulums are used in divination, dowsing, decision making, and solving mysteries. If you're feeling that your pendulum can do more, you're right. Much more exists than what can fit into neat categories. In this chapter, you'll learn that pendulums can be used to find someone's ground color, fix chakras, achieve goals, and descry past lives. Keep in mind that this chapter doesn't fully encompass all that your pendulum is capable of but brings to light how you can take the magic of your pendulum a step . . . or five further. The possibilities truly are endless, and they are unique to each person. There is more to learn, but here you will get an excellent start.

Determine an Energy Field

The human body, like everything else, is made of energy. An energy field consists of five layers: physical, etheric, emotional, mental, and spiritual. The closest layer we can detect is the physical, but the closer you get to a person, the closer you get to their other energy layers. It's best to picture the layers as energy radiating off of a person like an outline of their shape. In this spell, you'll determine how separated a person is from their energy field.

Gather:

♦ Pendulum
♦ A willing participant

1. Have your participant move around a little to loosen up, then walk them through your process of grounding and centering.

2. Ask them to stand with feet hip-width apart and to relax their shoulders. If they feel any resistance or hesitancy, their energy field can shrink.

3. Walk approximately 10 feet (3 m) away from the participant with your pendulum in hand.

4. Turn around and state your intention: *My intention is to find [person's name]'s physical energy field. Please react when I find it.*

5. When you come in contact with the field, your pendulum should noticeably react. Ask:

Ask

Please tell me when I reach the [etheric, for example] level.

6. Keep doing so until you've reached all levels. List the levels that registered strongly from further away from the person. These indicate aspects of their energy field that are separating from them.

7. Together, come up with a list of ways they can bring their energy closer and ask your pendulum if it will work for each option. For example, *Will daily meditation repair the energy field?* Or *Are there blocked chakras?* Now you'll know what they need to do to restore their field to perfect health.

Determine Ground Color

Colors are a huge part of our lives. They surround us and can project unspoken messages to others about how we view them and ourselves. A person's ground color is like their personality color. It's meant to reveal who they are and, some believe, can determine their path in life. In this spell, you'll determine your ground color (or another person's) and get insight into who you are. Some ground color meanings that might prove helpful are:

RED: leader, strong-willed, center of attention

PINK: romantic, gentle, childlike

ORANGE: social, youthful, vivacious

YELLOW: optimistic, independent, knowledgeable

GREEN: values all relationships, energetic, wise

BLUE: organized, calm, law-abiding

PURPLE: creative, unique, unconventional

BROWN: dependable, supportive, sincere

BLACK: rebellious, sophisticated, unassuming

WHITE: clean, bold, open-minded

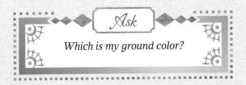

Gather:

♦ Pendulum
♦ Color Chart

1. Cleanse your pendulum, close your eyes, and take a deep breath. If you're doing this with someone else, have them mimic you.

2. Set up your Color Chart on a clean surface and hang your pendulum over the center of it. Ask:

Ask

Which is my ground color?

3. Use this answer to get a more complete view of yourself.

4. Surround yourself with this color frequently. A good way to stay grounded is to carry a ribbon or crystal in that color with you to promote daily spiritual stability.

Unblocking Chakras

On page 34 of this book, you learned that having blocked or unbalanced chakras can make us feel sick and unhealthy, so it's important to ensure that they flow freely. You can unblock them for yourself, but you can also help someone else who may not know how to do it. Using your pendulum, you can help restore them to their healthy, happy self.

Gather:

♦ Pendulum
♦ A willing participant
♦ A soft place to lie down

1. Have the person lie down flat on a soft surface. You want them to be comfortable and receptive to what you're about to do. Ask your pendulum:

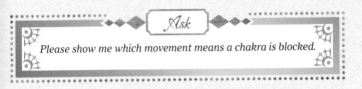

Ask

Please show me which movement means a chakra is blocked.

2. Begin with the root chakra and move upward (refer to pages 34–35 for the chakra locations on the body).

3. When your pendulum indicates unbalanced or blocked chakras, make note of them in your mind.

4. Tell the person to imagine a wheel on top of the corresponding chakra(s). Have them close their eyes and imagine the wheels slowly rotating until they feel a release and the chakras are clear. This is a cleansing visualization so go into great detail and take your time.

If you're doing this practice on yourself, use your Chakra Chart.

Communicate Telepathically

Nowadays, we can converse with anyone in so many ways—by direct message, mail, email, text, and phone, to name a few. But another way to do it is telepathically with your pendulum. You may want to get someone's attention without tipping off anyone else around them. Maybe you want to share secrets, or you might just want to open a line of communication. Using your pendulum, you can send messages discreetly.

Gather:

♦ Pendulum
♦ Meditative music (optional)
♦ Picture of the person you want to communicate with (optional)

1. Sit in a quiet space and take a deep breath or play meditative music (if using) so that you can clear your mind.

2. Envision the person you want to communicate with in your mind, or look at a picture of them.

3. Hang your pendulum over a cleared-off space, and set your intention by saying, *I intend to communicate with [person's name].*

4. Hold the image of the person in your mind and watch your pendulum until it moves in its positive response. When this happens, it means you've made contact.

5. Ask aloud or in your head:

Ask

[Person's name], can you please contact me?

6. Repeat the steps until the person you're trying to contact answers you.

7. If you've performed the ritual three times but you've heard nothing, assume that the person may be busy and will contact you later.

Descry a Past Life

We are one soul living multiple lifetimes, forgetting the past each time we're reborn. With your pendulum, in addition to some of your charts, you can gain insight into your past lives. It can be a lengthy process, so have some patience and be sure to record your answers.

Gather:

♦ Pendulum
♦ Numerical Chart
♦ Months Chart
♦ Days of the Week Chart
♦ Global map
♦ Alphabetical Chart

1. To begin you'll need to determine when your past life was born. Using the Numerical Chart, ask:

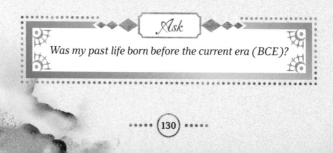

Ask

Was my past life born before the current era (BCE)?

2. Once you get the answer, you can determine the year. Ask:

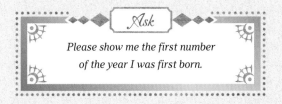

*Please show me the first number
of the year I was first born.*

3. Repeat until you get a full number. Earlier years can have as little as one or two digits. Your pendulum will give consistent negative answers once you have the full number.

4. To know the exact date you were past-born, pull out the Months and Days of the Week Charts, respectively, and ask:

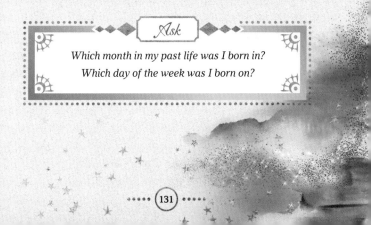

*Which month in my past life was I born in?
Which day of the week was I born on?*

5. Next, take out the global map and dowse over each country. Or take out the Alphabetical Chart and ask:

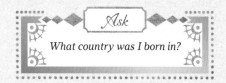

Ask

What country was I born in?

6. Now, once you have time and place, you can move to deeper questions to bring to light who you were. Some good examples are:

Ask

Did I reach adulthood?
Was I a crusader for justice?
Did I have children?

7. Sometimes, we have a significant other in our current life who we know we have a deep spiritual connection to. This can be a romantic partner, a sibling, a friend, or a parent. See if you knew them in your past life by asking:

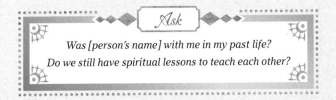

Ask

Was [person's name] with me in my past life?
Do we still have spiritual lessons to teach each other?

This is a very subjective practice, so it can lead you down many paths during your questioning. Most likely you've had more than one past life, so you can do this any time you feel called to. Examining a past life can bring great insight into your current one. It can help you focus on what you need to learn and how your soul needs to grow. It can also uncover lessons that you failed to learn in your previous earthly adventures and show you opportunities to learn that lesson in this one.

Recall Your Dreams

Dreams can tell us so much; for example, which decision to make, what might be lacking in our lives, or what Spirit has in store for us. Yet when we awaken, our dreams can vanish, like sand running through our fingers, and before we know it, the dreamscape is gone. Thankfully, there is a way for us to retrace our ethereal steps and unlock the secrets of our dreams.

Gather:

♦ Pendulum
♦ Pen and paper
♦ Yes/No Chart (optional)
♦ Amethyst (optional)

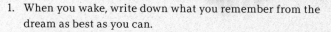

1. When you wake, write down what you remember from the dream as best as you can.

2. From here, set your chart (if using) on a clean, even surface. Then, take four deep breaths.

3. Hold your pendulum and ask:

Ask

Did the dream start where I recall it started?

Depending on your answer, you may ask something to the effect of:

Ask

Is what I remember of the dream accurate?

4. Keep asking questions and document the answers until the dream comes into full focus. Then, look at the themes and the elements that stand out to you the most. Ask Spirit what they are trying to tell you.

To encourage more messages, sleep with amethyst under your pillow.

Enhance a Tarot Reading

Tarot cards are a divination tool that has been around for centuries. With a mix of major and minor arcana cards, they can give insight into your past, present, and future. Because of their prevalence, a newbie may feel overwhelmed with all the steps it takes in order to perform a reading. But novice and expert alike can benefit from some pendulum enhancement.

Gather:

♦ Pendulum
♦ Tarot deck(s)
♦ Numerical Chart

1. If you've never bought a deck before, take your pendulum to your local metaphysical store and dowse over each deck to find the right one. Ask:

> ### *Ask*
>
> *Which deck is the most compatible with me right now?*

2. Shuffle your deck and spread the cards out across a clean space. Use your Numerical Chart and ask:

Ask

How many cards should I pull for this spread?

3. State your intention. Are you dowsing for romance, business, or a look into the future?

4. Pull and place that number of cards, face down, before you.

5. Dowse over each card, keeping the cards that your pendulum responds the most strongly to. Flip the remaining cards and use your intuition or interpretation book to read each card.

6. If you feel as though there's something missing, ask your pendulum specific yes/no questions over each card until you get the clearest message.

Purge Negativity

We all carry negativity with us, whether it's mental or physical. Everything can't always be positive. We're always going to have bad days, and despite our best efforts, we may hold on to negativity so long that it gets stuck in our bodies. You may experience symptoms like headaches, under- or over-eating, sleep problems, or anxiety. With this spell, you will begin to purge yourself of the negativity and free yourself from its bind.

Gather:

♦ Pendulum
♦ Fellow witch or trusted person
♦ A soft place to lie down
♦ An open window

1. Take four deep breaths alongside your trusted person so that you're both calm and your energies are in sync.

2. Lie down and relax your body. If you're tense, you'll block the pendulum's ability to show you the root of the problem.

3. Now, both of you say aloud in tandem: *Our intention is to find the negativity settled in [your name]'s body. Show us where the negativity lies.*

4. Have them start dowsing the pendulum at your feet and slowly move up until it gives a positive response.

5. Once you've got one, place your hands over the spot and ask aloud:

Ask

Spirit, can you please flow through me and purge me of this darkness?

6. Imagine the negativity flowing from your body into your hands, and then lift your hands up and away from you toward the open window.

7. Repeat steps 5 and 6 until you've purged every part of you.

Solving Family Arguments

Being a family means loving each other through thick and thin. But there are moments in between the joy when everyone's not on the same page. You may be experiencing the same arguments over and over again, or there's a lot of tension between everyone. Sometimes, the people involved don't even know why they're arguing anymore. This is where you come in and give each party insight and solutions.

Gather:

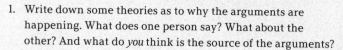

♦ Pendulum
♦ Pen and paper

1. Write down some theories as to why the arguments are happening. What does one person say? What about the other? And what do *you* think is the source of the arguments?

2. Dowse over each theory and ask:

Ask

Is this why [persons A, B and/or C] are arguing?

3. Dowse until you get a positive answer.

4. If you don't get a positive answer, use your intuition to develop more theories as your pendulum reveals more and more information.

5. When you've gotten to the root of the problem, it's time to look for solutions. Make a list of options, such as counseling, time apart, or letting the argument play out. Ask:

Ask

Is this the best solution for our family?

6. Repeat until you get the answer.

Note that you can't force anyone to do anything but use discernment to determine how big of a push your family might need.

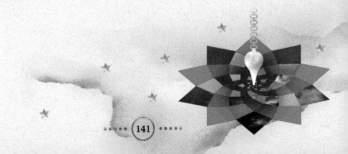

Manifest Your Goals

Actualizing a dream is something everyone should experience. The satisfaction of putting your mind to something and having it come true tastes so sweet. But having so many goals can be overwhelming. You may want to start your own business, visit a monument, run a marathon, or fly first class. Each goal, of course, requires its own unique steps, so it's good to narrow down those that are achievable for you right now. Your pendulum can help.

Gather:

♦ Pendulum
♦ Pen and paper
♦ Jasper quartz for motivation

1. Write down your list of goals. Be as honest as possible without thinking, *This would never work. I won't ever be able to do this.* This is not the right mindset for this spell.

2. Look at your list of goals to make sure they are coming from your heart—not from outside pressure.

3. Place the paper where you will see it every day for a week and add anything else that comes to you within that time.

4. Once the list is finalized, hover your pendulum over each goal and ask:

Ask

Am I ready to achieve this goal right now?

5. Envision what your life would look like if it were actualized.

6. If the pendulum says yes more than once, ask:

Ask

Is this the goal I should start with?

7. If yes, carry the jasper with you as you take the first steps toward achieving that goal or until it goal has been fulfilled.

Infuse Your Altar with Magic

In witchcraft, there's an array of spells we can participate in. Some are as simple as a thirty-minute spell, while others might take two hours. It all depends on the intention and intricacies of the spell. There are times when you might be feeling down or off-balance and you need some extra help. For this spell, you can use your pendulum to add a boost to whatever ritual you intend to perform.

Gather:

♦ Kyanite pendulum to radiate magic
♦ Incense
♦ Moonwater
♦ Altar

1. Cleanse your pendulum with incense smoke by swinging it through the plumes.

2. Let your pendulum charge under the moon overnight and leave water next to it to make moonwater.

3. Wash your hands with moonwater to both cleanse and charge them, then hold your pendulum in your hands to infuse it with your energy.

4. Place your pendulum on your altar and say this affirmation aloud: *I use this pendulum to add magic to my sacred space.*

5. Let your pendulum twirl all over the area you're going to utilize. Let it swing wide and free over the space.

6. When you're done, be sure to thank the pendulum before putting it away.

Cleanse Your Space

Energy outside the body is just as important as energy inside the body. Internally, we need to keep ourselves clear, but the spaces we occupy also need to be cleared of negative energy if we're to function at our best. As you move about, you may notice that your space feels off and you're not sure why. You may need to do a thorough cleansing with your pendulum to bring harmony back once again.

Gather:

♦ Amazonite pendulum to repel negative energy
♦ Incense or salt spray

1. In order to calibrate the pendulum, go into a space you know is energetically clean—an empty field or a smudged room, for example.

2. Note how the pendulum reacts in that place and use that as a barometer for other rooms.

3. Go into the space that needs cleansing. If it's a space like a home or an office, start with the entrance and go from room to room as you would naturally move about and state your intention: *I intend to completely cleanse this space with my pendulum.*

4. Open the windows to let out any negative energy.

5. Go from room to room and smudge the space as needed with the incense or salt spray. Hang your pendulum in each space and ask:

Ask

Is this space clean now?

6. Continue until the whole area is clean.

Meet Your Spirit Guides

A spirit guide is a universal force that helps us on our journey to become our Higher Selves. There are varying types of spirit guides: animals, trans-species (combining two or more species), angels, ancestors, shamans, plants, deities, ascended masters, and elemental spirits. It's believed that everyone is born with spirit guides—yes, plural. If we don't make an effort to see them, we may live our whole lives without ever benefitting from what they have to show us. In this spell, you will put yourself into a trance so you're in the right headspace to meet them.

Gather:

♦ Angelite pendulum for spiritual communication
♦ Incense
♦ Meditative music
♦ Alphabetical Chart (optional)

1. Use the incense smoke to clear the space. Perform your grounding practice or take four deep, cleansing breaths, swallowing several times to clear your throat chakra.

2. Turn on the meditative music and close your eyes. You want your mind to go into an alpha-wave state, the state associated with deep meditation, so your mind will be the most receptive. Then, state your intention: *I intend to meet my spirit guide right now.*

3. Swing your pendulum in front of you until you feel yourself going into a trance. Take your time, then when ready, ask:

Ask

Can you please show yourself to me?

4. Watch for any signs, like a sudden image in your mind, a sharp temperature change in the room, or a feeling across your skin.

5. When your guide has made contact, use your pendulum and Alphabetical Chart to ask questions, like what their name is. Let your intuition guide you through the rest of the session.

Connect to Your Higher Self

Your Higher Self is the part of you that exists outside the physical world. It's not burdened with the limitations you have, and it has wisdom that's specific to you. If you need insight into your current situation, you can always call on your Higher Self to give you guidance. Your Higher Self is different from a spirit guide because it is still you, not a separate entity.

Gather:

♦ Angelite pendulum for spiritual communication
♦ Meditative music
♦ Yes/No Chart (optional)

1. Turn on the meditative music and take four deep breaths to settle your mind.

2. When you're grounded and relaxed, hover your pendulum over your palm or Yes/No Chart and ask:

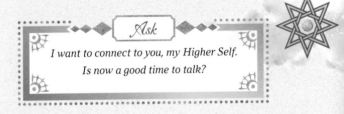

Ask

I want to connect to you, my Higher Self.

Is now a good time to talk?

3. If the pendulum says no, discontinue the ritual. If it says yes, then ask:

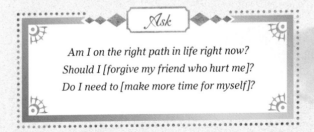

Ask

Am I on the right path in life right now?

Should I [forgive my friend who hurt me]?

Do I need to [make more time for myself]?

Rest assured that your Higher Self knows what's best.

Locate Your Spiritual Path

Our spiritual journeys are all different. But no matter the journey, we can all use some direction. For this spell, you'll use your pendulum to interpret angel numbers—signs from angels that are meant to show you where you are on your life's journey. They can be signs of encouragement, warnings, or assurances. With this spell, the angels will guide your pendulum to send you their important message.

Gather:

♦ Clear quartz pendulum for clear messaging
♦ Meditative music
♦ Blue lace agate for angel magic
♦ Numerical Chart

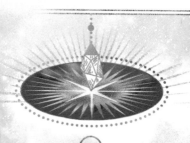

1. Because you'll be communicating with angels, it's best to get as close to being on their level as possible. Put on the meditative music, close your eyes, and breathe in deeply four times to raise your vibrations.

2. Place the Numerical Chart on a cleared-off surface and position the blue lace agate near it.

3. Hover your pendulum over the Numerical Chart and ask:

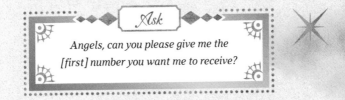

Ask

Angels, can you please give me the [first] number you want me to receive?

4. Here, you can either just make the first number you receive into a triple digit, then read your messages from there, or you can repeat step 3 three times.

5. When you're ready to decipher your message from the angels, hold the blue lace agate to your heart and first, thank the angels for their message, then ask them to guide your intuition when interpreting what they want you to know. Refer to the chart on pages 18–19 for a list of number meanings.

Conclusion

Pendulums are so much more than they appear to be. By now you've unlocked their power and are familiar with their abilities. Going forward, you and your pendulum(s) can develop a stronger connection, so you can perform even more spells that fit your specific needs. Though this book is comprehensive, magic is expansive. Create more charts or different types of pendulums as you see fit. As long as you follow your intuition and practice safely, you can do anything Spirit leads you to do.

Keep track of your questions, your answers, your charts, and everything else having to do with your pendulum for future reference. You want to build off of where you began to determine where you'll go. By documenting your journey, you can see how accurate your readings are, which pendulums are the most in sync with you, and what they (and you!) can do for others. From here, you can transcend the contents of this book.

You may want to develop an understanding of the different types of premade pendulums and what they can offer per spell or per day. Perhaps your next step is to explore the world of pendulum alchemy. Or you may find your calling with physical healing. Enter the spirit world and enhance your psychic abilities; there is always more to learn. Create abundance in your life. Do what you feel called to do.

With lots of practice, your pendulum will be an invaluable part of your magical toolbox, on its own or in concert with other divination tools and spells. From this moment on, you're in charge of your destiny and how far you want to take your pendulum(s) with you.

So mote it be.

Spell Index

3. Making Discoveries

4. Eclectic Magic

Inspiring | Educating | Creating | Entertaining

Brimming with creative inspiration, how-to projects, and useful information to enrich your everyday life, quarto.com is a favorite destination for those pursuing their interests and passions.

Library of Congress Cataloging-in-Publication Data

Names: Noir, Fortuna, author.
Title: Pendulum magic : an enchanting spell book of discovery and magic /
   Fortuna Noir.
Description: New York, NY, USA : Wellfleet Press, [2023] | Series: Pocket
   spell books; 6 | Includes index. | Summary: "With Pendulum Magic,
   discover the pendulum's power to act as your guide through the mystical
   world"-- Provided by publisher.
Identifiers: LCCN 2022040218 (print) | LCCN 2022040219 (ebook) | ISBN
   9781577153382 (hardcover) | ISBN 9780760379981 (ebook)
Subjects: LCSH: Fortune-telling by pendulum. | Pendulum--Miscellanea.
Classification: LCC BF1779.P45 N65 2023 (print) | LCC BF1779.P45 (ebook)
   | DDC 133.3/2--dc23/eng/20220914
LC record available at https://lccn.loc.gov/2022040218
LC ebook record available at https://lccn.loc.gov/2022040219

Publisher: Rage Kindelsperger
Creative Director: Laura Drew
Managing Editor: Cara Donaldson
Editor: Sara Bonacum
Text: Johanie M. Cools
Cover and Interior Design: Evelin Kasikov

Printed in China

Continue your on-the-go spellcraft with additional companions in the Pocket Spell Books series:

978-1-57715-314-6 978-1-57715-313-9 978-1-57715-312-2

978-1-57715-336-8 978-1-57715-339-9

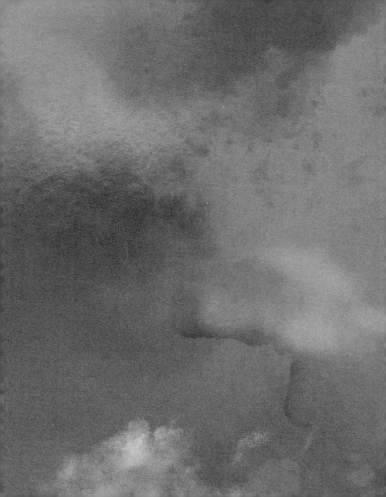